Small ways to do big things:

The Art of Micro-Actions, Unlocking Your Potential for Big Results.

Robert James

Table of Contents

Forward

Are you feeling stuck, overwhelmed, or unsure of how to achieve your goals? It's time to start taking small steps daily! Contrary to popular belief, it's not always the big leaps that lead to success. In fact, it's the consistent, daily actions that add up over time and pave the way for significant achievements. In this article, we'll explore how taking small steps daily can boost your confidence, make you more action-oriented, and help you connect the dots towards success.

Confidence is like a muscle that needs to be exercised regularly to grow stronger. When you take small steps towards your goals every day, you are consistently pushing yourself out of your comfort zone and building your self-belief. Each time you take action, regardless of how small it may seem, you prove to yourself that you are capable of making progress. This repeated success builds confidence and fuels your motivation to take more steps towards your goals.

Moreover, taking small steps daily helps you become more action-oriented. Instead of getting overwhelmed by the enormity of your goals, breaking them down into small, manageable tasks makes them more approachable. It's easier to take action when you have a clear plan and can focus on one step at a time. This mindset shift from looking at the big picture to taking small, actionable steps empowers you to be more proactive and take consistent action towards your goals, rather than getting paralyzed by the fear of failure or feeling overwhelmed by the magnitude of the task.

Additionally, taking small steps daily helps you to join the dots towards success. Success is rarely a straight line, but rather a series of interconnected dots. Each small step you take is a dot that connects to the next one, and over time, these dots form a meaningful pattern that leads you closer to your goal. By taking daily actions, you are consistently moving forward, building momentum, and creating a clear path towards your desired outcome. These small steps also allow you to learn from your experiences, make adjustments along the way, and optimize your approach, which ultimately increases your chances of success.

Chapter 1

Set specific and achievable daily goals.

Break down your bigger goals into smaller, actionable tasks that you can accomplish each day. This could be as simple as making a to-do list or setting a target for the number of steps you take towards your goal each day. Achieving our goals can be a daunting task, especially when they seem big and unattainable. However, the secret to achieving our goals lies in breaking them down into smaller, achievable daily goals.

Setting specific and achievable daily goals is a powerful strategy that can help us achieve our bigger goals with ease. By breaking down our goals into smaller, actionable tasks, we create a clear roadmap that helps us stay focused and motivated towards our end goal.

One way to set specific and achievable daily goals is to *create a to-do list*. This is a simple yet effective technique that can help us stay organized and productive throughout the day. By writing down the tasks that we need to accomplish, we create a visual reminder of what needs to be done, and we can track our progress as we complete each task.

Another way to set specific and achievable daily goals *is to set a target for the number of steps we take towards our goal each day*. For example, if our goal is to write a book, we can set a target of writing 500 words each day. This helps us stay focused on the process rather than the outcome, and it helps us build momentum towards achieving our bigger goal.

When setting daily goals, it is important to be realistic and avoid setting goals that are too ambitious or unrealistic. Setting goals that are too difficult to achieve can lead to frustration and demotivation, which can ultimately derail our progress towards our bigger goals. It is also important to celebrate our achievements and acknowledge our progress towards our goals. This helps us stay motivated and encourages us to keep pushing forward towards our end goal.

In conclusion, setting specific and achievable daily goals is a powerful strategy that can help us achieve our bigger goals with ease. By breaking down our goals into smaller, actionable tasks, we create a clear roadmap that helps us stay focused and motivated towards our end goal. So, start setting daily goals today and watch as you make steady progress towards achieving your dreams.

Create a daily routine

Unlocking Success: The Power of a Daily Routine

Are you struggling to make progress towards your goals? Do you feel like you're constantly spinning your wheels and not getting anywhere? If so, it's time to harness the power of a daily routine. Establishing a consistent routine that includes dedicated time for working towards your goals can help you build momentum, stay focused, and achieve success. In this article, we'll explore the benefits of a daily routine and how it can transform your life. Whether you're a busy professional, a student, or a stay-at-home parent, incorporating a daily routine into your life can be a game-changer.

The Importance of Consistency:
Consistency is the key to success. When you establish a daily routine, you create a sense of structure and order in your life. This consistency helps you stay on track and makes it easier to develop positive habits that align with your goals. Whether it's allocating 30 minutes every morning for

writing, reading, or exercising, consistency is what will keep you moving forward towards your aspirations. It's like building a muscle - the more you exercise it, the stronger it becomes.

Building Momentum:
One of the most significant benefits of a daily routine is that it helps you build momentum. Starting your day with a set routine helps you kickstart your productivity and sets the tone for the rest of the day. When you consistently work towards your goals every day, you begin to make progress and build momentum. This momentum propels you forward and makes it easier to stay motivated and focused. Soon, you'll find yourself making significant strides towards your goals, and the progress you make will inspire you to keep pushing forward.

Enhancing Productivity:
Productivity is crucial for success, and a daily routine can significantly enhance your productivity levels. When you have a dedicated time slot for specific tasks, you're less likely to procrastinate or get distracted. Instead, you'll be laser-focused on the task at hand, and you'll be able to accomplish more in less time. For example, if you allocate 30 minutes every morning for writing, you'll be amazed at how much progress you can make on your writing projects over time. A daily routine helps you make the most of your time and energy, making you more efficient and effective in working towards your goals.

Developing Positive Habits:
Habits are the building blocks of success. When you establish a daily routine, you're essentially creating a framework for developing positive habits. For instance, if you allocate 30 minutes every morning for exercising, you're not only making progress

towards your health and fitness goals, but you're also forming a habit of regular exercise. Over time, this habit becomes ingrained in your daily routine, and it becomes second nature to prioritize exercise in your life. Similarly, if you allocate time for reading or writing, you'll be developing habits that boost your knowledge and creativity. Positive habits are powerful tools for success, and a daily routine is the perfect way to cultivate them.

Managing Time Effectively:
Time is a precious resource, and a daily routine helps you manage it effectively. With a routine in place, you have a clear plan for how you'll spend your time each day. This helps you prioritize your tasks and ensures that you're dedicating time towards your goals consistently. A routine also helps you avoid wasting time on unproductive activities or getting overwhelmed by a lack of direction. When you know exactly what you need to do each day, you can make the

most of your time and make significant progress towards your goals.

Overcoming Challenges:
No journey towards success is without challenges. However, a daily routine can help you overcome these challenges more effectively. When you have a consistent routine in place, it becomes easier to stay focused and motivated, even when faced with.

Chapter 2

Practice self-reflection

How Celebrating Wins and Learning from Challenges Can Help You Achieve Your Goals

As we strive to achieve our goals, it's important to remember that progress is a journey, not a destination. Taking the time to reflect on our progress, celebrate our wins, and learn from our challenges can be a powerful tool in staying on track towards our goals. In this article, we will explore the benefits of reflection and how it can help you achieve success.

Celebrate Your Wins
Whether big or small, celebrating your wins is crucial to maintaining motivation and momentum towards your goals. Recognizing and

acknowledging your achievements, no matter how small they may seem, boosts your self-esteem and provides positive reinforcement for your efforts. It also helps you to appreciate your progress and the hard work you have put in.

Take the time to reflect on your wins, both short-term and long-term, and celebrate them in a way that is meaningful to you. It could be treating yourself to something you enjoy, sharing your achievements with loved ones, or simply taking a moment to pat yourself on the back. Celebrating your wins not only feels good, but it also helps to reinforce positive behaviors and encourages you to keep pushing forward.

Learn from Your Challenges
Challenges are inevitable on the path to achieving your goals. Instead of

seeing them as setbacks, view them as opportunities for growth and learning. Reflecting on your challenges allows you to gain valuable insights and identify areas for improvement.

When faced with a challenge, take the time to reflect on what happened, what you learned from it, and how you can apply those lessons moving forward. Did you encounter any obstacles or setbacks? What could you have done differently? What skills or knowledge can you develop to overcome similar challenges in the future?

Learning from your challenges helps you to become more resilient and adaptable, and equips you with the tools to handle obstacles more effectively in the future. It also allows you to make adjustments to your approach, ensuring that you are constantly improving and moving closer to your goals.

Make Adjustments and Stay on Track

Reflection is not only about celebrating wins and learning from challenges, but also about making adjustments to your strategy and staying on track towards your goals. Regularly assessing your progress and making necessary adjustments helps you to stay focused and aligned with your objectives.

Certainly! Let's dive deeper into the power of reflection by exploring some examples of how celebrating wins and learning from challenges can help you achieve your goals.

Example 1: Celebrating Wins
Imagine you set a goal to run a 5K race, and after weeks of training, you

finally complete your first race. It's a significant accomplishment, and taking the time to reflect and celebrate your win is crucial. You could celebrate by treating yourself to a massage, buying yourself a new pair of running shoes, or sharing your achievement with friends and family. By acknowledging and celebrating your win, you reinforce the positive behavior of consistent training and motivate yourself to continue working towards more ambitious goals, such as running a 10K or a half marathon.

Example 2: Learning from Challenges

Let's say you set a goal to launch your own business, and you encounter challenges along the way. Perhaps you face difficulties with marketing, struggle with cash flow, or experience setbacks in finding reliable suppliers.

Instead of being discouraged, you take the time to reflect on these challenges and learn from them. You analyze what went wrong, what you could have done differently, and what skills or resources you need to overcome similar challenges in the future.

Through this reflection, you identify areas for improvement and make adjustments to your business strategy. For instance, you might decide to invest in additional marketing efforts, streamline your cash flow management, or diversify your supplier network. By learning from your challenges and making necessary adjustments, you increase your chances of success and move closer to achieving your business goals.

Example 3: Making Adjustments and Staying on Track

Let's say you set a goal to improve your health and fitness by losing weight and becoming more active. After a few weeks of consistent exercise and healthy eating, you notice that your progress has slowed down, and you're struggling to stay motivated. Instead of giving up, you take the time to reflect on your progress and make adjustments to your approach.

You realize that you need more variety in your workouts and that you could benefit from working with a personal trainer to develop a more tailored exercise plan. You also identify that you need to plan your meals better to avoid temptation and stay on track with your healthy eating goals. With these adjustments in place, you regain your momentum and continue making progress towards your health and fitness goals.

In all these examples, the power of reflection is evident. By taking the time to reflect on your progress, celebrate your wins, learn from your challenges, and make adjustments as needed, you can stay focused, motivated, and aligned with your goals. Reflection provides you with valuable insights, helps you maintain a positive mindset, and ensures that you are continuously improving your approach. It's a powerful tool that can significantly contribute to your success in achieving your goals.

Take the time to review your goals and the progress you have made towards them. Are you making consistent progress? Are you facing any roadblocks? Are there any areas that require additional effort or resources? Reflecting on these questions allows you to identify any gaps and make adjustments to your approach as needed.

Remember, goal setting is not a one-time event but an ongoing process. By reflecting on your progress, celebrating your wins, and learning from your challenges, you can continuously refine your strategy and stay on track towards achieving your goals. In conclusion, the power of reflection cannot be underestimated in the pursuit of your goals. Taking the time to celebrate your wins, learn from your challenges, and make adjustments to your approach can significantly contribute to your success. So, as you work towards your goals, remember to set aside time for reflection. Reflect on your progress, celebrate your wins, and learn from your challenges. By doing so, you'll be well-equipped to overcome obstacles, stay motivated, and achieve the success you desire. Happy reflecting!

Chapter 3

Cultivate positive habits

Identify small habits that align with your goals and incorporate them into your daily routine. For example, if your goal is to improve your health, you could start by drinking more water, taking the stairs instead of the elevator, or going for a short walk after dinner.

For example, if your goal is to improve your health, you could start by drinking more water, taking the stairs instead of the elevator, or going for a short walk after dinner.

Transform Your Life Through Small Changes

In our fast-paced and busy lives, our habits play a significant role in shaping our overall well-being and success. Habits are behaviors that we repeatedly do without consciously thinking about them. They can either empower us or hold us back. The good news is that we have the power to cultivate positive habits that can transform our lives for the better.

In this chapter, we will explore the power of positive habits and provide practical strategies to help you cultivate and sustain them. Whether you want to improve your health, relationships, productivity, or overall happiness, this book will guide you on a journey of self-discovery and personal growth. Through small changes and consistent effort, you can transform your life and unlock your full potential.

We will delve into the science of habits and understand how they are formed and sustained. We will explore the concept of habit loops, which consist of a cue, routine, and reward, and how they influence our behavior. We will also discuss the neuroscience behind habits and how they are wired in our brains. Understanding the science of habits will provide you with a solid foundation to cultivate positive habits effectively.

Habits are not just random behaviors, but rather a series of interconnected processes that occur in our brains. Understanding the science behind habits can provide you with a unique formula to cultivate positive habits effectively. In this chapter, we will explore a practical and unique formula based on the latest research in behavioral psychology and neuroscience.

The Habit Loop Formula: **Cue - Routine - Reward - Belief**

The Habit Loop Formula consists of four key elements: **Cue, Routine, Reward, and Belief.** Understanding and leveraging these elements can help you create and sustain positive habits that can transform your life.

- **Cue:** The cue is the trigger that initiates a habit. It can be a specific time of the day, a location, an emotional state, or any other signal that prompts you to engage in a particular behavior. The cue can be as simple as sitting down to read a book, opening your Kindle app, or seeing your favorite genre of book cover.

Practical Tip: Identify the cues that trigger your negative habits, such as checking social media, snacking on unhealthy foods, or procrastinating, and replace them with cues that prompt you to engage in positive habits, such as placing a book in a visible location, setting a reminder on your phone, or creating a reading routine at a specific time of the day.

- **Routine:** The routine is the actual behavior or habit that you engage in as a response to the cue. It can be a physical action, a mental process, or an emotional response. For example, the routine can be reading a chapter of a book, highlighting important passages, or taking notes while reading.

Practical Tip: Experiment with different routines and find the ones that work best for you. For example, you can try different reading techniques, such as skimming, scanning, or active reading, and see which one enhances your comprehension and enjoyment of the book.

- **Reward:** The reward is the positive outcome or benefit that you receive from engaging in the habit. It can be a sense of accomplishment, a feeling of pleasure, or a tangible reward, such as a treat or a break. The reward can be gaining knowledge, escaping into a captivating story, or simply enjoying the process of reading.

Practical Tip: Identify the intrinsic and extrinsic rewards that you can associate with your positive habits. For example, you can reward yourself with a healthy snack, a short walk, or a social media break after completing a chapter of a book. Also, focus on the long-term benefits of the habit, such as personal growth, improved skills, or enhanced well-being, to motivate yourself to continue the habit.

- **Belief:** The belief is the mindset or attitude that you hold about the habit. It can be positive or negative and can influence your motivation, confidence, and persistence in cultivating the habit. The belief can be the conviction that reading is a valuable and enjoyable activity that contributes to personal growth and fulfillment.

Practical Tip: Cultivate a positive belief system around your habits by challenging and changing any negative thoughts or beliefs that may be holding you back. Develop a growth mindset, where you see habits as opportunities for learning, improvement, and self-mastery. Surround yourself with positive influences, such as books, articles, or people who inspire and motivate you to cultivate positive habits.

Understanding the science of habits and leveraging the Habit Loop Formula - Cue, Routine, Reward, and Belief - can provide you with a practical and unique formula to cultivate positive habits that can transform your life. By identifying the cues, routines, rewards, and beliefs associated with your habits, you can make intentional changes to create positive habits that contribute to your personal growth, well-being, and fulfillment.

Identifying Your Current Habits.

Take a closer look at your current habits and assess their impact on your life. We will explore how to identify your habits and categorize them into positive, negative, and neutral. We will also discuss how habits are interconnected and how changing one habit can create a ripple effect in other areas of your life. This chapter will help you gain self-awareness and identify which habits you need to cultivate or eliminate to achieve your desired outcomes.

The UNIQUE Formula:

We will introduce a unique formula that will guide you in identifying your current habits and assessing their impact on your life. The UNIQUE formula is a practical and actionable approach that will help you gain clarity and insight into your habits, enabling you to make informed decisions on which habits to cultivate or eliminate to achieve your desired outcomes.

1. *Understand the Habit Loop:* The first step in the UNIQUE formula is to understand the habit loop, which consists of a cue, routine, and reward. Cues are triggers that initiate the habit, routines are the actions or behaviors that make up the habit, and rewards are the positive outcomes or benefits that reinforce the habit. By understanding the habit loop, you can identify the cues, routines, and rewards associated with your habits and gain awareness of their underlying patterns.

2. *Note Your Habits:* The next step is to take note of your habits. Keep a habit journal or use a habit tracking app to record your habits for a week or two. Be honest and detailed in your observations. Note down the habits that you engage in regularly, both positive and negative, and the circumstances or situations that trigger them. This will help you create a comprehensive list of your habits and gain a deeper understanding of your behavioral patterns.

3. *Identify the Impact:* Once you have listed your habits, the next step is to assess their impact on your life. Evaluate each habit based on its positive or negative impact on various aspects of

your life, such as health, relationships, productivity, finance, and personal growth. Reflect on how each habit aligns with your values, goals, and vision for your life. This evaluation will help you identify which habits are supporting your well-being and which habits are holding you back from reaching your full potential.

4. *Uncover the Triggers:* The fourth step in the UNIQUE formula is to uncover the triggers or cues that initiate your habits. Cues can be internal or external, such as emotions, time of day, location, or specific people or situations. Reflect on the cues associated with each habit and write them down. Identifying the triggers will help you become more aware of the

situations or circumstances that prompt your habits, and enable you to take proactive measures to modify or eliminate them if needed.

5. *Quantify the Habit:* The next step is to quantify your habits. Measure the frequency, duration, and intensity of each habit. For example, if you want to cultivate a positive habit of exercising, note down how often you exercise, how long you exercise, and the intensity of your workouts. This will help you gain a clear understanding of the current state of your habits and track your progress as you work towards cultivating positive habits.

6. *Explore Alternatives:* The sixth step in the UNIQUE formula is

to explore alternatives to your negative habits. Reflect on the underlying needs or cravings that your negative habits fulfill and brainstorm healthier alternatives that can meet those needs. For example, if you have a habit of stress-eating, you could explore alternative coping mechanisms such as mindfulness, exercise, or talking to a friend. This will help you identify positive habits that can replace your negative habits and fulfill the same needs or cravings in a healthier way.

7. In conclusion, using the UNIQUE formula - Understand the Habit Loop, Note Your Habits, Identify the Impact, Uncover the Triggers, Quantify the Habit, and Explore Alternatives - will provide you

with a systematic approach to identify your current habits and assess their impact on your life. This self-awareness will empower you to make informed decisions on which habits to cultivate or eliminate to create positive changes in your life. By understanding the unique dynamics of your habits, you can take proactive steps towards transforming your habits and ultimately, transforming your life for the better.

Chapter 4

Setting Meaningful Goals

The Unique Formula for Success

The importance of setting meaningful goals that align with your values and vision for your life cannot be underestimated. You've probably learnt the concept of setting *SMART* goals (Specific, Measurable, Achievable, Relevant, and Time-bound) and how to set realistic and achievable goals. We will also discuss how to create a plan and track your progress to ensure that you stay on track and motivated.

Setting meaningful goals will provide you with a *CLEAR* roadmap to cultivate positive habits and make lasting changes in your life. Now I will introduce a unique formula that will guide you in setting and achieving your goals effectively. This formula, called the "*CLEAR*" formula, is a practical and compelling approach that will help you create goals that are aligned with your values and vision, and set you up for success.

C - Clarify Your Vision: The first step in setting meaningful goals is to clarify your vision. What is it that you truly want to achieve? What are your core values and aspirations? Take the time to reflect on your dreams, desires, and what truly matters to you. Be specific and clear about what you want to accomplish, and ensure that your goals are in alignment with your overall vision for your life. For example, if your vision is to live a healthy and active lifestyle, your goal could be to exercise for 30 minutes daily.

L - List Your Goals: Once you have a clear vision, list down your goals. Start by brainstorming and writing down all the goals that come to mind, regardless of how big or small they may seem. This will help you get a comprehensive overview of what you want to achieve. Then, review your list and prioritize your goals based on their significance and feasibility. Select the goals that are most meaningful to you and that you believe you can realistically achieve within a specific timeframe. For example, if your goal is to improve your relationships, you could list down goals such as spending quality time with loved ones, improving communication skills, and resolving conflicts peacefully.

E - Establish SMART Goals: Once you have identified your goals, it's essential to establish SMART goals - Specific, Measurable, Achievable, Relevant, and Time-bound. Specific goals are clear and well-defined, measurable goals can be tracked and evaluated, achievable goals are realistic and within your reach, relevant goals align with your vision and values, and time-bound goals have a deadline. Applying the SMART criteria to your goals will help you set clear and actionable goals that are more likely to be achieved. For example, instead of a vague goal like "get fit," a SMART goal could be "exercise for 30 minutes daily, five days a week, for the next three months."

A - Create an Action Plan: Once you have established SMART goals, the next step is to create an action plan. Break down your goals into smaller, manageable steps or milestones that you can work on daily or weekly. Create a timeline and schedule specific actions that will help you progress towards your goals. Be realistic and flexible in your planning, and anticipate potential challenges or obstacles that may arise along the way. For example, if your goal is to read 20 books in a year, your action plan could include scheduling time for reading, setting a target number of pages or chapters to read daily, and tracking your progress.

R - Review and Reflect: Regularly review and reflect on your goals and progress. Assess how well you are doing in achieving your goals and whether any adjustments or improvements are needed. Celebrate your achievements, no matter how small, and use setbacks or failures as opportunities to learn and grow. Reflect on your motivations, obstacles, and strategies, and make necessary changes to your action plan if required. For example, if you missed a week of exercise due to a busy schedule, reflect on what happened, adjust your schedule, and recommit to your goal.

The CLEAR formula is a powerful and practical guide to setting meaningful goals that will help you cultivate positive habits. By clarifying your vision, listing your goals, establishing SMART goals, creating an action plan, and regularly reviewing and reflecting on your progress, you will be well-equipped to achieve your desired outcomes and transform your life.

Creating a Habit-Forming Environment

Now we will explore how your environment influences your habits and how you can design your environment to support your desired positive habits. We will discuss how to eliminate triggers or cues that lead to negative habits and how to create new cues that prompt you to engage in positive habits. We will also discuss the importance of social support and accountability in cultivating positive habits. Creating a habit-forming environment is a unique formula for success and will provide you with the necessary support and structure to make positive habits a natural part of your daily routine.

- **Step 1:** *Identify Your Habit Triggers*
  The first step in creating a habit-forming environment is to identify the triggers or cues that prompt your current habits, whether they are positive or negative. Triggers

can be anything from a specific location, time of day, emotional state, or even the people you are with. Take some time to reflect and make a list of the triggers that are associated with your current habits. For example, if you tend to snack on unhealthy foods when you're stressed, the trigger may be stress or a particular location, such as your office or living room.

- **Step 2:** *Eliminate Negative Triggers*
  Once you have identified the triggers associated with negative habits, it's essential to eliminate or minimize them from your environment. This may involve making some intentional changes, such as removing unhealthy snacks from your pantry or finding ways to manage stress effectively, such as practicing mindfulness or engaging in physical activity. By eliminating negative triggers, you are reducing the likelihood of engaging in those habits

and creating a space that supports positive habits.

- **Step 3:** *Create Positive Triggers*
The next step is to create positive triggers in your environment that prompt you to engage in your desired habits. Positive triggers are cues that make it easy for you to remember and initiate your positive habits. For example, if you want to cultivate a habit of exercising in the morning, you can set out your workout clothes the night before or place your exercise mat in a visible spot in your home. This will serve as a reminder and make it easier for you to start your exercise routine in the morning.

- **Step 4:** *Establish a Daily Routine*
Establishing a daily routine can significantly contribute to creating a habit-forming environment. Having a consistent routine helps your brain

develop a pattern and makes it easier to form and sustain habits. Plan out your day, including the time slots for your desired habits, and stick to it as much as possible. For example, if you want to make reading a daily habit, schedule a specific time each day to read, such as before bed or during your lunch break. Consistency is key in forming positive habits, and a daily routine can provide the structure you need to make your habits stick.

- **Step 5:** *Surround Yourself with Supportive People*
  The people you surround yourself with can have a significant impact on your habits. Surround yourself with individuals who support and encourage your positive habits. Share your goals and progress with them, and ask for their support and accountability. Having a supportive community can keep you motivated,

provide fresh perspectives, and hold you accountable to your desired habits.

- **Step 6:** *Track Your Progress*
Tracking your progress is a powerful motivator in cultivating positive habits. Keep a record of your habit-building journey by using a habit tracker or journal. Track each time you engage in your desired habits and celebrate your successes. Seeing your progress visually can be incredibly rewarding and reinforce your motivation to continue cultivating positive habits.

Creating a habit-forming environment is a unique formula that can set you up for success in cultivating positive habits. By identifying your habit triggers, eliminating negative triggers, creating positive triggers, establishing a daily routine, surrounding yourself with supportive people, and tracking your progress, you can create an environment that fosters positive habits and supports your journey towards personal growth and transformation.

With these practical and compelling strategies, you can unlock your full potential and make a positive impact on your world.

Practicing Habit Stacking and Habit Substitution

Two powerful strategies for cultivating positive habits - habit stacking and habit substitution. Habit stacking involves attaching a new habit to an existing habit that you already do consistently. We will explore how to identify existing habits that can serve as anchors for your new positive habits. Habit substitution involves replacing a negative habit with a positive habit that fulfills the same need or craving. We will discuss how to identify the underlying needs or triggers of your negative habits and find healthier alternatives to meet those needs.

Practicing habit stacking and habit substitution will help you seamlessly integrate positive habits into your daily routine.

Habit Stacking: Building New Habits on Existing Ones

Habit stacking is a simple yet effective strategy that involves attaching a new habit to an existing habit that you already do consistently. By leveraging the power of an existing habit, you can easily integrate a new positive habit into your routine without relying solely on willpower or motivation. Here's how you can create your unique formula for habit stacking:

Step 1: *Identify an Existing Habit*
Think about a habit that you do consistently every day, such as brushing your teeth, making your bed, or brewing your morning coffee. This will serve as your anchor habit,

the one that you will stack your new habit onto.

Step 2: *Choose a New Habit*
Next, choose a new positive habit that you want to cultivate. It could be a habit related to your health, productivity, personal growth, or any other area of your life that you want to improve. For example, if you want to incorporate exercise into your routine, your new habit could be doing a quick 10-minute workout or going for a short walk.

Step 3: *Attach the New Habit to the Existing Habit*
Now, simply attach your new habit to the existing habit. For instance, if you chose to do a quick workout, you could do it right after brushing your teeth in the morning or before making your bed. The key is to make the new habit immediately follow the anchor habit without any extra effort or decision-making.

Step 4: *Repeat and Track Your Progress*
Consistency is key in habit stacking. Repeat the new habit after the anchor habit every day until it becomes automatic. Track your progress and celebrate small wins along the way to stay motivated and reinforce the habit loop. With time, your new habit will become second nature, and you can move on to stacking more positive habits onto your existing routine.

Habit Substitution: Replacing Negative Habits with Positive Ones

Habit substitution is another powerful strategy that involves replacing a negative habit with a positive habit that fulfills the same need or craving. This allows you to address the root cause of the negative habit and create healthier alternatives. Here's how you can create your unique formula for habit substitution:

- Step 1: *Identify the Negative Habit and Its Trigger*

Take a close look at a negative habit that you want to eliminate from your life, such as snacking on unhealthy food when stressed, procrastinating when facing a challenging task, or scrolling through social media when bored. Identify the triggers or cues that prompt you to engage in the negative habit, such as stress, boredom, or fatigue.

- Step 2: *Identify the Underlying Need or Craving*

Dig deeper and identify the underlying need or craving that the negative habit fulfills. For example, if you snack on unhealthy food when stressed, the underlying need may be to cope with stress or seek comfort. If you procrastinate when facing a challenging task, the underlying need may be to avoid discomfort or fear of failure.

- Step 3: *Find a Healthier Alternative Habit*

Next, find a positive habit that can fulfill the same need or craving in a healthier way. For instance, if you snack when stressed, you could replace it with a healthier alternative such as taking a short walk, doing deep breathing exercises, or talking to a friend.

Overcoming Common Challenges and Staying Motivated

We will address common challenges that you may encounter while cultivating positive habits and provide strategies to overcome them. We will discuss how to deal with setbacks, overcome self-sabotage.As we journey through life, we often encounter challenges that can hinder our progress and dampen our motivation. Whether it's pursuing a personal goal, striving for career advancement, or embarking on a creative endeavor, challenges are inevitable. However, with the right mindset and strategies, you can overcome these challenges and stay motivated on the path to success. We will explore some of the common challenges people face and provide practical tips on how to overcome them and maintain your motivation.

1. *Procrastination: The Productivity Killer.*

   Procrastination is a common challenge that many people struggle with. It's easy to fall into the trap of putting off tasks or delaying important decisions. However, procrastination can seriously hinder your progress and drain your motivation.

   To overcome procrastination, it's important to identify the root causes. Are you overwhelmed by the task at hand? Are you lacking clarity on what needs to be done? Are you afraid of failure or success? Once you understand the underlying reasons for your procrastination, you can take steps to address them.

Break down tasks into smaller, manageable steps. Create a to-do list and prioritize your tasks. Set deadlines for yourself and hold yourself accountable. Visualize the benefits of completing the task and imagine the satisfaction and sense of accomplishment you will feel. Surround yourself with a supportive environment and seek help or guidance when needed. By taking these steps, you can increase your productivity and motivation.

2. *Self-Doubt: The Confidence Crusher*
Self-doubt can be a significant challenge that can sabotage your motivation and hinder your success. It's natural to have moments of self-doubt, but allowing it to linger can be detrimental to your progress.
To overcome self-doubt, it's essential to cultivate self-confidence. Focus on

your strengths and achievements rather than dwelling on your weaknesses or failures. Challenge negative self-talk and replace it with positive affirmations. Surround yourself with supportive and encouraging people who believe in you. Set realistic goals and celebrate your progress along the way. Remember that everyone makes mistakes, and failure is a part of the learning process. Embrace failure as an opportunity to learn and grow, rather than a reason to doubt yourself.

3. *Lack of Motivation: Reigniting Your Fire*

   Loss of motivation is a common challenge that can occur at any stage of your journey towards success. It's normal to experience fluctuations in motivation levels, but it's crucial to find ways to reignite your fire and keep moving forward.

One effective way to regain motivation is to ***revisit your "why."*** Remind yourself of your purpose and the reasons behind your goals. What drives you? What do you hope to achieve? How will it benefit you and those around you? Reflecting on your deeper motivations can reignite your passion and fuel your determination. It's also essential to set short-term and long-term goals. Short-term goals provide immediate gratification and a sense of accomplishment, while long-term goals keep you focused and provide direction. Celebrate your achievements, no matter how small, to maintain momentum and motivation.

Additionally, consider changing your environment or routine to break up monotony and rekindle your motivation. Surround yourself with inspirational and like-minded individuals, seek out new challenges, and step out of your comfort zone. Remember that motivation is not always constant, and it's okay to have off days. Be kind to yourself and practice self-compassion.

4. *Time Management: Maximizing Your Productivity*
Another common challenge that can hinder success is poor time management. Many people struggle with juggling multiple responsibilities, tasks, and commitments, which can lead to a sense of overwhelm and decreased motivation.
To overcome time management challenges, prioritize your tasks.

Chapter 5

Seek support

Finding Strength in Community

In life, we all face challenges and obstacles that can leave us feeling overwhelmed and alone. Whether it's dealing with a personal loss, navigating a difficult decision, or coping with mental health issues, facing these struggles on our own can be incredibly daunting. However, there is a powerful tool that we often overlook: seeking support.

As human beings, we are inherently social creatures. We thrive on connection and community. When we face adversity, turning to others for support can make a world of difference. In this article, we will explore the importance of seeking support and how it can positively impact our lives.

One of the key aspects of seeking support is recognizing that it's okay to ask for help. Many of us are conditioned to believe that asking for help is a sign of weakness or failure, but this couldn't be further from the truth. In fact, reaching out for support takes courage and vulnerability. It's a brave act that acknowledges our limitations and the need for assistance. It's important to remember that we are not meant to navigate life's challenges alone, and seeking support is a natural and healthy part of the human experience.

Support can come in many forms. It can be from friends, family, mentors, or even professional help from therapists or counselors. The key is to find the right type of support that meets your needs. It's okay to explore different options and try different avenues until you find what works best for you. It's important to remember that seeking support is not a sign of weakness, but rather a sign of self-care and self-awareness.

One of the most powerful benefits of seeking support is the validation and perspective it can provide. When we share our struggles with others, we often find that we are not alone. Many people have faced similar challenges and can offer empathy, understanding, and valuable advice. Hearing different perspectives can also broaden our own views and help us see our challenges from different angles, which can lead to fresh insights and solutions. In addition to emotional support, seeking support can also provide practical assistance.

For example, if you're facing a difficult decision, talking it through with a trusted friend or mentor can help you weigh the pros and cons and gain clarity. If you're coping with a loss, seeking support from a grief support group can provide you with coping strategies and tools to navigate through the grieving process. Support can come in many forms, and the right support system can make a tangible difference in our lives.

Furthermore, seeking support can also foster personal growth and resilience. When we face challenges and receive support, we learn to develop coping skills, problem-solving strategies, and emotional resilience. We become better equipped to handle future challenges and setbacks, knowing that we have a support system in place to lean on when needed. Seeking support can also help us gain a better understanding of ourselves, our values, and our needs, which can lead to personal growth and self-improvement.

In today's digital age, seeking support has become even more accessible. Online communities, forums, and support groups provide virtual spaces for people to connect and seek support from others who may have similar experiences. Social media platforms allow us to reach out to friends and family, even if they are far away. The internet has made it easier than ever to find support and connect with others, regardless of location or time zone.

Seeking support is a powerful and necessary tool for navigating life's challenges. It's important to remember that *asking for help is not a sign of weakness*, but rather a sign of strength and self-awareness. Support can come in many forms, from emotional to practical, and can provide us with validation, perspective, and tools for personal growth.

Unlocking Success Through Collaboration

In a world that often celebrates the lone wolf, the self-made success story, and the rugged individualist, it's easy to fall into the trap of thinking that we must go it alone in order to achieve big things. However, the truth is that seeking support from others can be a powerful tool for unlocking success and achieving our goals. In this article, we will explore why seeking support is not only necessary but also essential for doing big things, and how collaboration can be the key to unlocking our fullest potential. One of the most significant misconceptions about success is that it's a solitary journey. Many believe that in order to achieve greatness, we must isolate ourselves from others, keep our ideas secret, and work tirelessly on our own. However, this mindset can be detrimental to our progress. Seeking support from others doesn't make us weak; it makes us smart.

First and foremost, seeking support provides us with a fresh perspective. When we work in isolation, we can become blinded by our own biases, limited by our own experiences, and trapped in our own echo chamber. By seeking support, we open ourselves up to new ideas, feedback, and insights that we may have never considered on our own. Collaborating with others allows us to tap into their unique perspectives, experiences, and expertise, which can lead to innovative solutions and breakthroughs that we could never achieve on our own.

Moreover, seeking support creates a network of allies who can help us navigate challenges and overcome obstacles. No matter how talented or capable we are, we all face setbacks and difficulties along the way. Having a support system in place can provide us with the encouragement, motivation, and accountability to keep going when the going gets tough. It's like having a team of cheerleaders who are invested in our success and who can provide us with the support we need to persevere, even in the face of adversity.

Furthermore, seeking support can also open doors and create opportunities that we may not have access to otherwise. Networking and building relationships with others can lead to collaborations, partnerships, and introductions to influential individuals who can help us advance our goals. By leveraging the power of our networks, we can tap into a world of resources, knowledge, and connections that can propel us forward in our journey to do big things.

It's important to note: *that seeking support doesn't mean relinquishing control or giving up on our own capabilities. It's not about being dependent on others or relying solely on their efforts. Rather, it's about recognizing that we are stronger together than we are alone.*

Collaboration allows us to combine our strengths, leverage our collective skills, and amplify our impact. It's about finding the right people who complement our abilities, challenge our thinking, and help us become better versions of ourselves.

Rising Together: Finding Support to Achieve Big Dreams

Many people have big dreams, but they often face obstacles that seem insurmountable without the right support system. In today's fast-paced world, it's easy to feel overwhelmed and isolated in our pursuit of big dreams. Whether you're aspiring to start a successful business, write a best-selling book, or make a difference in your community, the journey can be challenging. However, the good news is that you don't have to do it alone. Seeking support from others can be a game-changer that propels you towards success.

One of the most powerful ways to find support is by forming a mastermind group. A mastermind group is a gathering of like-minded individuals who come together to support and encourage each other in their respective endeavors. These groups are often formed around a specific topic or goal, such as entrepreneurship, personal development, or creative pursuits. They meet regularly to share ideas, insights, and resources, and hold each other accountable for taking action towards their goals.

Being part of a mastermind group can be incredibly empowering. It provides a sense of community, camaraderie, and shared purpose. You can bounce ideas off each other, brainstorm solutions to challenges, and learn from each other's experiences. Moreover, the diverse perspectives and skills of the group members can open up new possibilities and opportunities that you may not have considered on your own. It's a true testament to the old saying, "Two heads are better than one."

Another way to seek support is by finding mentors or coaches who can guide you on your journey. Mentors are experienced individuals who can provide valuable advice, guidance, and wisdom based on their own experiences. They can help you navigate challenges, offer insights, and provide a different perspective on your goals. Coaches, on the other hand, are professionals who can provide structured guidance, feedback, and accountability to help you achieve specific goals. Whether it's a business coach, life coach, or career coach, having someone in your corner who believes in you and your dreams can make a world of difference.

In addition to formal support systems, it's also crucial to cultivate a supportive network of friends, family, and colleagues. Surrounding yourself with positive, like-minded individuals who believe in your dreams can be incredibly motivating and inspiring. They can provide emotional support, celebrate your wins, and offer encouragement during challenging times. Having a strong support network can boost your confidence, keep you motivated, and help you stay focused on your goals.
Finally, it's important to remember that

support is a two-way street. Just as you seek support from others, be willing to offer your support to those around you. Be a cheerleader for others' dreams, provide encouragement, and offer your skills and resources when needed. Collaboration and mutual support can lead to incredible outcomes that benefit everyone involved.

In conclusion, achieving big dreams is not a solitary journey. It's about rising together with the support of others who believe in your vision. Whether it's through a mastermind group, mentors, coaches, or a supportive network, seeking and giving support can be a game-changer on your path to success. So, don't be afraid to ask for help, and be willing to offer your support to others as well. Together, we can achieve extraordinary things and make our dreams a reality. So, let's rise together and make our mark on the world!